Comments on other *Amazing Stories* from readers & reviewers

"Tightly written volumes filled with lots of wit and humour about famous and infamous Canadians."
Eric Shackleton, *The Globe and Mail*

"The heightened sense of drama and intrigue, combined with a good dose of human interest is what sets Amazing Stories *apart."*
Pamela Klaffke, *Calgary Herald*

"This is popular history as it should be... For this price, buy two and give one to a friend."
Terry Cook, a reader from Ottawa, on **Rebel Women**

"Glasner creates the moment of the explosion itself in graphic detail...she builds detail upon gruesome detail to create a convincingly authentic picture."
Peggy McKinnon, *The Sunday Herald*, on **The Halifax Explosion**

"It was wonderful...I found I could not put it down. I was sorry when it was completed."
Dorothy F. from Manitoba on **Marie-Anne Lagimodière**

"Stories are rich in description, and bristle with a clever, stylish realness."
Mark Weber, *Central Alberta Advisor*, on **Ghost Town Stories II**

"A compelling read. Bertin...has selected only the most intriguing tales, which she narrates with a wealth of detail."
Joyce Glasner, *New Brunswick Reader*, on **Strange Events**

"The resulting book is one readers will want to share with all the women in their lives."
Lynn Martel, *Rocky Mountain Outlook*, on **Women Explorers**

THE HEART OF A HORSE

AMAZING STORIES

THE HEART OF A HORSE

Poignant Tales and Humorous Escapades

ANIMAL/HUMAN INTEREST
by Gayle Bunney

PUBLISHED BY ALTITUDE PUBLISHING CANADA LTD.
1500 Railway Avenue, Canmore, Alberta T1W 1P6
www.altitudepublishing.com
1-800-957-6888

Extreme care has been taken to ensure that all information presented in
this book is accurate and up to date. Neither the author nor the
publisher can be held responsible for any errors.

Publisher   Stephen Hutchings
Associate Publisher   Kara Turner
Editor   Frances Purslow

We acknowledge the financial support of the Government
of Canada through the Book Publishing Industry Development
Program (BPIDP) for our publishing activities.

Altitude GreenTree Program
Altitude Publishing will plant twice as many trees as were used
in the manufacturing of this product.

National Library of Canada Cataloguing in Publication Data

Bunney, Gayle, 1954-
Heart of a Horse / Gayle Bunney

(Amazing stories)
ISBN 1-55153-994-2

Horse--Anecdotes. 2. Bunney, Gayle, 1954- --Anecdotes. I. Purslow,
Frances. II. Title. III. Amazing stories (Canmore, Alta.)
SF301.B852 2003   636.1   C2003-910419-2

An application for the trademark for Amazing Stories™
has been made and the registered trademark is pending.

Printed and bound in Canada by Friesens
4 6 8 9 7 5

For two young horse lovers who have worked beside me out in the horse corrals. While learning about the care and control of our faithful friend, the horse, they gave me joy and laughter and made me young at heart again. Thank you, Amanda Wager and Travis Minor.

The author getting ready for another day of ranch work.

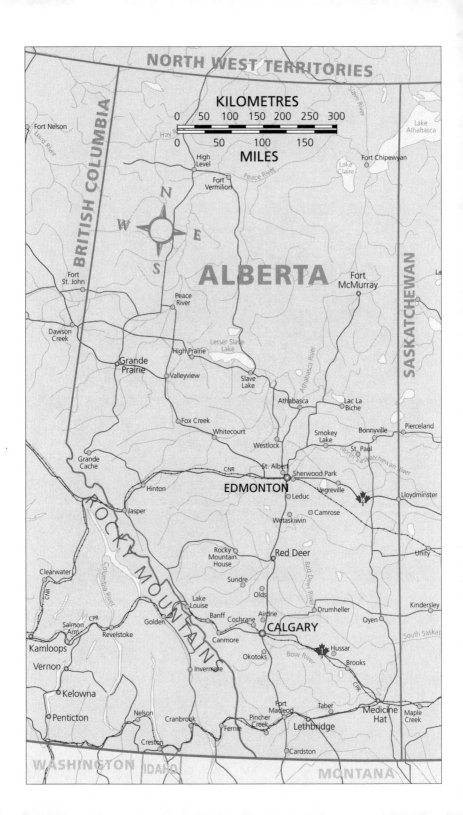

Contents

Prologue 15

Chapter 1 Flashlights and Glowing Eyes 17

Chapter 2 The Horse That Came To Stay 21

Chapter 3 Herman 30

Chapter 4 Lost Trust 36

Chapter 5 What Are Friends For? 48

Chapter 6 The Power of Love 58

Chapter 7 The Mare Who Got
                  into the Whisky Barrel 63

Chapter 8 Stormy's Donkeys 66

Chapter 9 A Case of the Strangles 71

Chapter 10 Cow Tales 74

Chapter 11 Old Flip 83

Chapter 12 Lights Out! 91

Prologue

Today is already cracking up to be just another typical day at my acreage. One of my many dogs woke me early by placing two muddy paws on my forehead. The farrier arrived ahead of schedule to trim the horses' feet and put an end to my morning coffee. After catching and tying the first half dozen horses along the fence for him, I thought fleetingly about eggs and toast, but a gelding that hasn't recovered after a complicated surgery needed to be doctored first.

The farrier is fast and, by the time I put away the vet supplies, is patiently waiting for more horses to be caught. My stomach makes its first loud complaint, but a man coming to purchase one of my two year olds is expected before noon, and I want to trim its mane before he arrives. I might as well catch the well-trained sorrel at the same time. I will saddle both of them. I suspect after the buyer has ridden both the green colt and the trained sorrel, he may cough up the extra money to buy the super quiet sorrel that doesn't need weeks' more training.

The farrier trudges by me, halter in hand. He will catch the old broodmares himself. It's probably quicker than waiting on the owner, who is having trouble catching the well-trained but wild-eyed and snorting sorrel.

The Heart of a Horse

I shake the buyer's hand as he gets out of his truck and head him towards the main corral. I wonder why he gives me such an odd look. I turn to write out the cheque for the farrier. A man of few words, the farrier slips silently into his truck. But he can't resist. Rolling his window down, he says what he has secretly been wanting to say all morning: "Why do you have two perfect muddy paw prints on your forehead?" And you know what? It's not even noon yet.

Chapter 1
Flashlights and Glowing Eyes

 am late getting out to do the night grain feeding for the horses. They stomp and nicker as I head towards the corrals. I inch my way towards them, trying not to trip in the dark on the dozen excited miniature dogs around my feet.

Sure enough, my toe lands on someone's tail and the horrendous screeching that ensues makes my hair stand on end. I mutter that I should have docked its tail as a puppy so things like this wouldn't happen. I reach the light pole and flip the switch. Instantly the yard lights up. But five steps from the power pole, I hear a strange sizzling sound overhead. Two more steps and with a distinct popping sound, the yard light burns out, plunging me back into total darkness. Oh great, just great.

After fumbling with the safety chain on the main corral gate, I get it open and am met with a pen full of hungry weanlings pushing around me. I assure them that since they have the best of hay in front of them 24 hours a day, I doubt very much being two hours late with their grain is going to kill them. In response, one stud colt nips me smartly on the sleeve, managing to get some of my skin, too. Now I am showing the dog with the sore tail what real screeching sounds like. Ouch, that hurt. If I knew for sure which colt had done the dirty deed, I would bite him back.

The weanlings are all fed and accounted for. Both stallions are fed and accounted for. The mares and fillies are fed but I have to recount because one appears to be missing in the dark. Three recounts and one is definitely missing. It is a black yearling filly. No normal yearling would ever be off by herself. An old mare may go off by herself in the pasture, but not a young horse out of sight of the herd unless…. Lord, she is either sick or tangled in a fence. Back to the house on the double for a flashlight.

Strangely the pack of dogs only follow me as far as the pasture gate, then they beat it back towards the house. Man's best friend just deserted me. I head out down the centre of the pasture, stopping to call the filly's name and listen for any sounds in return. No whinnies, no twanging wire, no soft thud of hooves, nothing.

Halfway across the pasture, the thin beam of the flashlight picks up the glint of eyes to the south. I steady the light on the eyes. The filly must be lying down judging from the height of the glowing eyes off the ground. Speaking quietly, and pointing the light towards the ground to avoid panicking her, I head towards the filly. After several yards, I again shine my light towards her to make sure I am heading in the right direction. Suddenly, the glowing eyes go straight up in the air. "That's good," I think. "She can't be too sick if she can get to her feet." I turn off the flashlight because her head held up that high may be a sign she's getting spooked. I sure don't want her to turn and hit the fence behind her.

I walk more slowly, almost singing a flow of gentle words to keep her calm and let her know she has nothing to fear. Because I am forced to zigzag around rocks and dips in the land, I chance another quick look at her with the light. She is lying down again. This is not good at all. But wait! If she is lying down how come she is moving towards me? Now her glowing eyes have shot straight up in the air again. All of a sudden she is back down again. What is going on? That is the last time I eat four-day-old pizza for supper. My brain must be suffering from some kind of food poisoning.

Suddenly from the north side of the small pasture, comes the crashing of an animal charging through the willows. I am consumed by fear — fear of the approaching glowing eyes and fear of the animal careening towards me. I am frozen to the spot, as frozen as a turkey in the deepfreeze waiting for Thanksgiving.

Just then, the owner of the glowing eyes decides to give a warning woofing noise. Lord Love-a-duck, it's a bear! Scant yards in front of me, and coming my way. I realize that when those glowing eyes went high in the air, it was the bear rearing up on his hind legs to better see the idiot human walking straight to his waiting jaws. From the north comes the shrill whinny of the frightened missing yearling.

This frozen turkey suddenly sprouts wings, and I am out of there. I fly over the ground, going wide open. But the bear is gaining on me fast. I hear his thundering stride, and I'm terrified that I'm not going to make it back to the safety of the yard. It's all over. The open gate looms before me, but I can feel the bear gaining on me. I try for one last burst of speed.

As the black filly passes me and swerves through the gate ahead of me, I no longer hear the thunder of the charging bear's feet behind me. Silly me, since when do bear paws go "clippity clop, clippity clop?" Obviously, the bear couldn't be bothered to try and catch this frightened morsel of chicken.

Chapter 2
The Horse That Came to Stay

S ocks was a pretty nice gelding. Nice enough that buyers were always interested in him. That made my job of buying, training, and selling a whole lot easier.

I had purchased him as an unhandled two year old. His only close contact with humans had been getting dumped on the ground, gelded, and branded. He was a bit wild-eyed in the sale ring and scruffy enough looking that I didn't have to go overboard on the price paid for him. Once home, I gave him a healthy dose of dewormer, some good quality feed, and in no time he was looking pretty sharp. He took to being halter broke like a mouse to church on Easter Sunday. He took to the first saddling like he was born to wear a saddle. He took to training like a dog takes to a bone. He was good enough quality to keep around for a full year and finish his training.

But Socks had some annoying habits. Although he was as gentle as a kitten, he always managed to step on my toes — especially if I went to the corrals wearing running shoes instead of boots. The pain is more intense with only $9 running shoes between you and the horse's hoof instead of a pair of sturdy cowboy boots. As well, he always decided to bite at that horsefly on his side just as I was bending down to pick up a front hoof to clean it. WHAM! When our heads connected, I was the loser. Also, he'd pass wind when I was brushing out his tail. The smell was not pretty, if you get my drift.

Within a year, he was not only well trained but also gentle, with no spook in him. He was ready for me to find him a new home with a loving family. He may never be a great rope horse or a real humdinger of a cow horse, but he was a good all-around using horse. A pleasure to own and ride.

I soon sold him to a young fellow who seemed very excited to buy him. He loaded easily into the excited young fellow's rented stock trailer and except for stepping on my foot again when I was tying him in it, everything went smoothly. I stood on one foot and waved the other one in the air trying to kill the pain while we shook hands and promised to keep in touch. Socks had found his new home.

Within a month the fellow phoned me up. Yes, Socks was a nice horse. Yes, he liked Socks. But, he had found a motorcycle for a really good price and had put a down payment on it. Now he needed to sell Socks in a hurry, to get the rest of the money for the motorcycle. Could I possibly buy Socks back? Being the nice person that I am, I of course said, "No!"

The young fellow developed a slight whine to his voice, and said he would throw in the saddle, blanket, bridle, and the leftover square bales he had bought for Socks — all for the same price he had paid for him. Now, I was willing to deal.

When the young man pulled the horse trailer into my driveway, he was excited about making it to the "two-wheeler dealer" before closing time to pay for his new toy. I opened the end gate of the trailer and Socks nickered a welcome. I untied him and let him step out of the trailer, careful to keep my feet out of the way. He was fat and sassy, with no blemishes. Everything was fine.

It looked like there were at least 20 square bales of hay in the front compartment of the trailer, which I knew would come in handy. I barely had time to glimpse the saddle stuffed up on top of the stacked hay, when the budding biker dude danced in front of me needing his money to get to that dealership in time. I unloaded everything on the double, before handing him his money. He twirled in mid-air and flew down my driveway, tires squealing.

A more thorough inspection of the gear brought disappointment. The bridle was one of those old, wide leather-cheeked ones, with a rusted bit attached to it, worth about $5 if I could find someone to buy it. The saddle blanket had been left somewhere for mice to chew, but would do for a blanket in the corner of the barn for the cats to sleep on. The saddle was ancient — the leather was dried out from never being cared for, the cinch was toast, and the stirrups were missing. I wondered how much Socks was ridden, if his owner used a saddle with no stirrups. At least I got 20 bales of hay out of the deal. The next morning when I cracked open one of those puppies, I discovered it was mildew and mould from one end to the other. It was bonfire time!

Socks settled right in as if he had never left the place. I assured him he was not going to be around long. I took a quick spin on him, and he was as good as gold except for jarring my teeth when he decided to jump a 2-foot-long twig lying on the ground. I figure he cleared that monster twig by a good 4 feet.

A couple of weeks later, he loaded into a young couple's trailer without a care in the world. I let the man load him and made a mental note that Socks never even came close to stepping on his foot. The pretty little woman was already happily planning what toys and treats she would buy for her first horse. Socks was about to be spoiled big time.

Two months later, I again got the phone call. Yes, they loved Socks dearly. He was such a sweetie — their pride and joy — but he acted up something awful when she rode him. After falling off him twice, she was afraid to get back on him. Closing my eyes, I asked what Socks was doing. He fussed and reared, bucked, and jumped sideways. This didn't sound like the horse I knew. The husband got on the line and said that since I had a good reputation as an honest horse dealer, he knew I wouldn't mind taking Socks back. I had obviously sold them a horse that wasn't safe for his wife. I liked the good reputation part and the honest part, but I was having a problem with the buying him back part. Nonetheless, I gave in.

Socks pranced out of their trailer as fat as a hog. His eyes were lit up, and he was ready to do the cha-cha-cha. The little lady slipped him a handful of treats, as she produced his feeding schedule. I was still gazing at the list as they drove away. It included all the second-cut alfalfa hay he could eat, 10 pounds of special rolled, steamed oats/corn with molasses for breakfast, and the same again for supper. He liked his treats at noon, especially the sugar-coated ones made with bran. Just before bed, he needed sliced carrots and apples, or he couldn't sleep.

I led Socks down to the back pasture. He danced around, as charged as a highly fed racehorse on the way to the starting gate. I was glad I wasn't trying to ride him as he reared a couple of times and kicked out in sheer joy with his back legs. He was fat and sassy. He was what I call "out of his cotton-picking mind" from an overload of energy-producing grain. I knew that some time out on pasture with nothing but grass to eat would settle him down. And he'd lose that roll of fat around his middle, too.

About three miles up the road lived two little blond girls with their dad. They spent a lot of time at my place on weekends, cleaning a box stall or two in exchange for riding my quiet horses. Socks soon became their favourite mount. Never once did he step on their cute little cowboy boots or even come close to tossing his head around them. I had let them bridle him with close supervision, and he patiently lowered his head way down for them. He even opened his mouth wide for the bit. Shucks, they could brush his tail, and he never passed gas either. In fact, he was ever so careful with his new friends.

The girls worked hard on their father, begging for the right to own Socks. Dad finally relented, and they rode Socks double down the driveway, waving back at me as they headed for home with their new horse. I waved back, secretly praying that I had seen the last of Socks.

He was back three days later, eating grain out of a sack in the back of my truck that he had ripped open with his teeth. He had obviously escaped somehow. Being full-grown, I refused to cry. Cowgirls don't cry!

I was faced with a dilemma. The father was one of the hardest working men I knew. He was raising these two wee ones as a single parent. He was a dairy farmer working long hours on his own. He would likely not even have noticed Socks was gone and even if he had, I doubted he would find the time to come get him. The girls would be in school. Worse, the family had no telephone, so I had no way of letting them know where the horse was. I was in-between horse trailers and using stock racks on the back of my truck. I was not about to load those racks for a horse needing to go only 3 miles. I nabbed Socks, bridled him, and rode him home bareback. Hopefully, the father was around the barns somewhere and could drive me back to my place.

We made good time, and I soon loped into their yard. A quick look around showed the open gate that Socks must have flipped the latch up on and escaped. I put him back in the corral, found some binder-twine and tied the gate shut. The father was nowhere to be found. I started walking home. Surely someone would come along and offer me a ride.

I arrived home with good-sized blisters on both heels from walking so far in riding boots. They were not meant for walking, they were meant for fitting snugly in stirrups.

Socks showed up again the following Monday. I rode him home again bareback wearing my $9 running shoes just in case. When I returned the escapee, the father informed me the girls were fighting over Socks every night after school. I just studied the tips of my running shoes and was thankful the horse hadn't stepped on my feet.

The next week, we went through the same routine, and the father said his daughters were worried that Socks kept running away because he didn't like them. He added that the girls were also upset because Socks refused to travel at anything but a slow walk with them. What a switch from the last owners' complaint!

The next morning when I found Socks adding fertilizer to my lawn, I was thinking about moving right out of the country so Socks couldn't find me. Just then, a beat-up, old truck and trailer rumbled up my driveway. When the driver stopped and got out, I flew into his arms, bouncing off his tremendous belly. We laughed and hugged while I asked, "What in the holy horrors of Hell are you doing here in this part of the country?" The old boy burped and belched a couple of times and happily informed me that he was looking for a place to rest up for a couple of days. Maybe do some work on his truck. I'm thinking he needs a lot of work on his truck, but I keep that to myself.

Now, this old sport is one of my heroes. He has seen more horses come and go than a dog has fleas. Yup, he's an old-time horse dealer from way back. He taught me that the customer always comes first. While you gotta make a profit, don't be lying to people. Those same people will come back and buy another horse from you years later, if you treat them right. Those same people will give your name to other potential customers, if you're honest. If you're not, they will give you a lot of other names besides the one you answer to.

In his trailer he had two of the cutest bay geldings I have ever seen. Just little guys, about 14 hands high. We chatted about them as we put them in the corral. Jimmy and Jolly had a bit of age on them, but they were real sweetheart kids' ponies. He had picked them up dirt cheap at an estate sale a couple of hundred miles back down the highway.

On the way into the house, we passed Socks nibbling on my kitchen windowsill. I managed to keep from cursing and explained my problem.

The next day, when the girls and their father came to get Socks, they fell in love with the matching bays. It was a match made in heaven — a horse for each of them that would be happy to stay put on their father's farm. My friend was happy with the straight across trade, and I was rid of Socks once and for all. Now if I could just get over missing him, I'd be fine.

Chapter 3
Herman

Back in the good old days, I began my career hauling horses with home-built stock racks on the back of an ancient 1957 Fargo. That truck and I were both stout, stocky, and built low to the ground. Neither of us was known for a whole lot of speed, but put us in mud up to our kneecaps and we could chug through it. We were both known to be hard to get started in the morning, but once going, we could go all day and night with just a shot of fuel every few hours.

When the day came to upgrade to my very first two-horse trailer with matching truck, things took a drastic turn for the worse. The horses that had always loaded so easily in open stock racks didn't take kindly to narrow, enclosed two-horse trailers. Some of my older saddle horses either refused to load or put up such a fight that I was late getting to where I was going most of the time. I figured either I had to go back to using the stock racks or buy new saddle horses.

The new horses weren't much better. The ones that really irked me were the horses that loaded fine on the outward journey, but then wouldn't load to come home again. I missed a lot of suppers because of that narrow horse trailer. Eventually, I figured I was going to have to go back to the "pain-in-the-butt-to-get-on-the-truck" stock racks, or upgrade to a bigger trailer.

The bank lent me the money and I came home with my new stock trailer. Now I could haul four full-sized horses or six little guys, and the horses loved the wide-open back of it.

With the ability to haul so many horses on one trip, I figured I should upgrade my horse operation and start buying and selling more horses. Maybe I could even go into raising the varmints on a bigger scale, besides I needed to turn over more horses to make my monthly trailer payments.

The bank manager frowned a little more than the last time, but finally coughed up a livestock loan so I could increase my number of horses. I was in heaven. This cowgirl was going into big time horse ranching. I would no longer have to work a job in town or ride for some other guy to make ends meet; now I could just hit the road buying and selling, while also increasing my broodmare band numbers.

While I was busy expanding my business, my husband

was getting cranky over me not having time to cook and clean anymore. The divorce wasn't a particularly nasty one. He got the farm and I got the stock trailer, the truck, and the horses. But I had to sell most of the horses to pay off my bank loans, and I needed to buy a new truck to replace the dud that I was driving.

And that's how I met Herman. I fell in love with him the first time I saw him 20 years ago. He was something to see when he was young, and he's still going strong to this day. Herman is a blue 1983 F150 4 x 4 Explorer with a strip of white down his side, and he's still my all-time favourite travelling companion. It's the longest lasting relationship I've had in my life. Herman and I have had some interesting experiences hauling horses together.

One time we headed out on a 16-hour round trip to deliver a horse to the racetrack. I had loaded a gelding to keep the nervous race mare company, and I had also loaded a friend into Herman's cab, to keep me from being too nervous about sending my mare to another person to finish training and race.

We delivered the racehorse and were on our way home. I was getting tired.My friend had never pulled a stock trailer in her life, especially not one with a horse loose in it, but I tried to talk her into driving for a couple of hours. A nervous Nellie, her biggest concern was what if a deer jumps out on the road?

"There are only two things you have to remember,"

I said. "First, you don't worry about the first deer you see crossing the road in your headlights, because it will continue across. It's the deer probably following it that you don't want to hit. Second, you have a live animal back there in that stock trailer, so don't lock your breaks up tight or you will knock the hell out of it. The horse is going to get hurt if it's slammed around in that trailer."

She was not convinced, but I couldn't finish a 16-hour drive. Right about the time I started yammering at her again, the first mule deer appeared in my headlights. True to form, the deer paused only for a second and continued across. As I predicted, the second one appeared from the ditch. I let off the gas and started breaking gently. The second deer continued across. The third appeared, making a mad dash to follow the others. Well, I didn't lock the brakes up real tight, to protect the loose horse in the back, but Herman tried to kiss that deer's rear end before coming to a full stop.

Right then, my nervous friend refused to drive at all. I cranked Herman's radio up full blast, rolled down the window and started singing to keep myself awake. My friend claims she sustained ear damage from the radio and a long-lasting headache from my singing.

It was about a year before I convinced her to come on another horse hauling expedition. This time we were heading out to buy some mares. In the wee hours of the morning, I backed Herman up to the trailer hitch. My friend dropped the ball into place while I dozed in the cab. She quickly went to the house for the thermos of coffee and snacks, while I did my usual trailer check. Hitch done up, safety chains done up, lights working, breaks working. The usual. I thought I had everything in order before climbing back into the truck for 30 more seconds of snooze time.

We were barrelling down the highway at pretty much warp speed since the trailer was empty, there was no other traffic, and Herman was feeling his oats. I was driving with one hand, and had a cup of coffee in the other. My friend munched on a banana for breakfast. Suddenly, with a violent jerk, Herman was thrown to the right. Then Herman was thrown to the left. In my usual calm way, I held my coffee cup out to my friend, "Hold my coffee, please. I think Herman blew a rear tire or something." She reached out and took my cup. Even with my two hands on the steering wheel, Herman leapt sideways.

Then for a split second, everything seemed to be under control, as we both watched a stock trailer much like ours sail past us on the passenger's side. I calmly said, "Boy that trailer looks a lot like mine."

My friend responded by throwing her hands up and screeching, "You idiot, that is your trailer!" as the trailer in question cratered in the ditch.

After that episode, Herman needed repairs to his rear end. The safety chains had destroyed the back of the truck when the trailer jumped off the ball, because it wasn't closed properly. I was just mad about the coffee and banana dripping down off the roof of the cab. The rest was fixable, but those stains are still there. What on earth was she thinking when she threw her hands up in the air like that?

Chapter 4
Lost Trust

What would it be like to lose all trust in others? What if you lost all capacity to care? To feel anything? What if you just gave up? That is what it was like for the old gelding. He was brought down so low by human hands, that he lost the ability to trust, care, or feel.

I didn't want to buy him. It was just one of those things that happens. I had made the long drive to a working cattle ranch to buy a registered quarter horse mare that was advertised for sale.

Like many such ranches, each and every animal must earn its keep in order to stay there. The mare had been one of their better cattle horses for a few years, but after tangling with a barbed wired fence, she became too crippled for riding. Always on the lookout for good broodmare prospects, I had been happy to find her quality bloodlines offered at a very reasonable price. Although not sound for riding, she'd be fine raising colts.

The ranch buildings were set back about a half mile off the main gravel road. As I ambled the old truck and trailer down the lane, I admired the black-and-white cows and their chubby calves grazing the pasture to my left. A hayfield to my right lay newly mowed, drying in the sun. I inhaled deeply to capture the smell of newly cut hay wafting into the truck cab through the open windows.

As I approached the house and yard, I noticed a half dozen saddle horses grazing in a smaller pasture, fat and content with life.

The rancher met me with a smile on his sun-crinkled face, a trusty, old red handkerchief hanging out of his back pocket. In a deep voice he asked, "You the girl come to look at the mare?" I nodded and he continued, "You don't look old enough to be raising horses." Now I grinned too. I was well into my 20s at the time, and he thought I was still just a girl. Shucks, he had just made a friend for life.

Two horses lounged in their corral in the shade of the big, red, hip-roof barn. The man passed the sorrel gelding without a glance, heading towards the mare. As I went past, I did a quick appraisal on the gelding. He was up there in age, with lots of old saddle sores from an ill-fitting saddle. He'd seen lots of feed but was not overly fat; his legs were clean of any serious blemishes. He had a roughly done brand on his hip, and although his head wasn't real pretty, it wasn't bad either. But when I looked into his eyes, I was startled. They were lifeless — totally devoid of anything. To me, a horse's eyes tell a million tales. They can show kindness, bad temperament, concern, fear, love, intelligence, or lack of it. But his eyes were blank slates. He didn't even acknowledge my presence, as his head remained lowered and motionless.

"Just a plug," said the man. I turned my attention to the mare and immediately liked what I saw. She was a stout mare with good withers; all-around good quarter horse conformation. Her pretty head had appealing eyes. Only her legs showed why so many horsemen dread that ripping death called barbed wire. Any horse that gets tangled in it and fights to free herself, will be left with serious scars. The mare was no exception. A slight limp on the left hind leg showed why she was no longer capable of being a saddle horse.

I ran my hands over her, starting on the left side. She tensed for a second as I examined her legs, then she relaxed. Moving around behind her, I found her to be straight legged, with no conformation faults in the hind end at all. As I moved up on the right side of her, I came within touching distance of the gelding. Impulsively, I reached out and stroked his nose. He never moved a muscle; he didn't even blink; yet I had given no warning that I was about to touch him. He should have raised his head, taken a step back, or otherwise reacted to my reaching out towards his face without warning.

Intrigued at this behaviour, I asked, "What is with this horse? It's as if he died, but forgot to fall down." And so I heard the story of Prince, the name I chose for him.

The rancher who now owned him was the proud grandpappy of a young boy who lived just up the road a piece. The rancher and his son worked the ranch together, the pair of them riding fence lines, doctoring cattle, rounding them up, and in the spring, calving them out. Since his grandson was old enough to sit on the back of a horse (about three years old, he proudly informed me), he and his trusty pony come with them on the shorter day rides. Now the boy's legs had grown too long for the pony, so Grandpappy decided to buy him his own full-sized horse. The horses they already owned were just a hair too much for the little fellow to handle yet.

One Friday he decided to attend a horse sale a couple of hours from home. Arriving at the auction, he toured the pens out back, searching for just the right horse. Like most small town auction sales, the pens were filled with basically undesirable horses. Most were untrained or poorly training at best; several had obvious soundness problems — the old and the just plain unwanted.

Then he spied the sorrel gelding. Saddled and bridled, ready for the ring, the horse stood quietly and patiently. A rather loud man was busy pointing out all the good things about the gelding to another potential buyer. The horse was the best. The quietest. Never bucked, never shied. You could ride him all day and all night and he would never quit on you. This gelding was the best kid's horse he had ever owned.

Now the rancher had been around a few years and was not fooled by all the promises. After all, if the gelding was that great, why was he at a small town monthly auction sale? Prices were always less at these sales than what a man could get for a good horse right at home in his own yard. Something was not being told by the loud, obnoxious man.

After the sale had started, the rancher quietly left the side of the ring to take another look at the gelding. Finding the gelding's pen vacant of the owner, he gave the horse a quick check for soundness. It appeared to be sound in every way. Raising the horse's head, he looked at its teeth to check its age. The horse was around 15 years old. Still, a 15- or 16-year-old horse was okay for his grandson, since the boy would not be riding and working him hard. At least the horse was super quiet, so he wouldn't have to worry about the boy getting hurt.

Later when the gelding and his rider entered the sale ring, the rancher spotted right off that the horse did not neck rein very well, nor did he seem to want to move any faster than a slow walk. The owner had to slap him hard with the ends of the reins to get a bit of animated speed out of him. Still, the gelding was sound and he did want a quiet horse for the boy. His was the final bid.

After paying for the horse, he brought his truck and trailer around to the loading area. On the way back to the pens to collect his new purchase, he passed the owner carrying his saddle over one shoulder. Stopping the man, he said, "Before the sale, you mentioned that your gelding was a good children's horse. How old were the kids that were riding this horse, and how much horse experience did they have?"

The seller shrugged, "Young kids, adults, old ladies, city slickers — they all rode this horse, and very few had any horse experience. I run a dude ranch in the foothills. You don't have anything to worry about with that gelding." With that, he shifted the weight of the saddle to his other shoulder and walked away.

While the rancher was telling me this story, I stroked the mare and watched the gelding. Twice a buzzing horsefly attacked him, but he never so much as flinched. He made no attempt to bite it, kick at it, or even switch his tail at this vicious little monster. Yet when the horsefly switched its attack to the mare, she responded like any horse does — with frustration and every attempt to get it off her. What was wrong with this gelding anyway? It was as though he felt nothing, reacted to nothing. I couldn't figure him out.

The man chuckled, "You came to buy the mare, but all you do is stare at that plug. When you pulled in the yard, my missus would have put the coffee on and I'm willing to bet, found us something to snack on too. We best go in and sample whatever she's put out for us."

I soon decided you would have a hard time meeting nicer people than this man and his bubbly wife. The coffee was the real McCoy — brought to a boil on top of the old gas stove in its pot with a blackened bottom from years of use. The cream was thick and rich, and came straight from a four-legged milk machine. The apple pie was to die for, so I wasn't in any hurry to go home. Contentedly, we moved to the veranda to sip another cup of coffee, while I coaxed him into continuing the story of the gelding. From here, I could still watch the horse, and I noticed that since we were no longer in the corral with him, he was fighting off those darn horse-flies like a normal horse. His head had come up a couple of notches, and he looked more alert. It was the strangest transformation.

The rancher continued his story. When he got the sorrel home from the auction, he cleaned him up, trimmed his mane and feet, and called his son to bring the boy for a visit. The youngster stared at his new horse, eyes big with wonder. A full-sized horse all his own. He loved his fat pony, but he imagined a big horse would be even more fun. He pressed his cheek to the gelding's nose as his grandpa made sure the small saddle fit the gelding's back properly. With a bridle in place, he was ready for his first ride on his very own big horse.

The first problem surfaced immediately. He wasn't tall enough to get his foot in the stirrup to pull himself up. A boost from his dad was ever so embarrassing for this young cowboy. With his father on one side of him and Grandpa on the other in case the gelding did something wrong, he clucked to the gelding to move on out. Nothing happened.

He kicked with his little heals, clucked like mad, and the gelding finally shuffled into gear. Around and around the pen they ambled, the gelding never so much as flicking an ear. After Dad and Grandpa made two trips around, they were satisfied that the gelding was indeed gentle, so they leaned against the rails. "Kick him into a trot," called the boy's father.

He tried. He kicked and clucked and shouted, "Giddy up!" But the gelding continued his slow walk. He slapped the horse with the ends of his reins, just like he sometimes had to do with his pony, but the horse plodded on. Disappointment set in pretty quick.

The next day the three of them saddled up to check a distant pasture of cows. They usually travelled at a fast trot or lope to get where they were going in good time. The boy was soon in tears. Kicking, begging, slapping with the reins produced a slow, pathetic trot that had him falling behind the men, who had to stop and wait for him. The gelding refused to turn anywhere, insisting on following right behind the other horses.

He was an unhappy boy by the time they got back to the barnyard. He wanted his jolly, chubby pony that always did what he asked of her. Grandpa didn't blame him in the least.

The rancher saddled up the gelding himself the next day to find out if he was just a plug or simply taught to go slowly with kids on him. Surely he would liven up with an adult giving the directions.

But the rancher was angry, exhausted, and ready to

shoot the gelding by the time he returned home. Only by spurring hard, something he hated doing, could he get any speed out of the plug. It was as if the gelding just didn't care. He refused to put any life into what was being asked of him.

The rancher's son rode the gelding for the next couple of weeks, as the boy didn't want to. It was a constant battle to get the horse to put some energy into what was asked of him. Finally, he told his father to can the horse, as it wasn't worth the effort.

And that was why the gelding was in the corral with the mare now. The meat horse buyer was expected to show up tomorrow or the next day, getting a liner load ready for a trip to the slaughterhouse. The rancher wouldn't make his money back on the gelding, but he wanted him gone from his property. He figured the horse wasn't worth the grass it took to feed him. I decided to take him off his hands.

I loaded the mare in the front compartment of my stock trailer and Prince in the back. I was hoping there really was a "prince of a horse" hidden inside that gelding somewhere.

Since I had never encountered a horse like Prince before, I chose to keep him in a holding area, where I could observe him for awhile in with some young geldings I was training. He acted just like any other horse, as long as I was nowhere near him. He established himself high in the pecking order with the others, quite able to lunge with ears back at any horse that trespassed in his space. He galloped around with them when the wind came up, just like a normal horse.

However, when I approached the pen, he became a motionless, unblinking, unhearing object. He just stood there, with no life in him at all. He never looked at me; he was a statue with head half hanging. He didn't even chew, for Pete's sake, when I was anywhere near him.

He was not a victim of severe abuse, as he did not flee from me, tremble, become tense, or hold his head high in fear. He was sound, and was not in any pain. He was normal in all respects as long as I wasn't near him. I decided he was a nutcase, pure and simple. Strange indeed.

I worked with horses to help make a living and except for the ol' faithfuls, who had been with me for many years, they came and went as soon as they were trained enough to sell. When I started riding Prince, I found the rancher's story to be true to a tee. I tried a soft colt Bosal, in case it was the bit he feared. No change. I tried riding him bareback in case saddles hurt his back. No change. I tried using strong leg pressure, blunt spurs, and tapping him with a whip with a popper on the end so it made more sound than sting. I spanked his butt with the long colt reins, in an attempt to liven him up. No change. And like the rancher and his son, I gave up. He continued to fascinate me, but it was time to find him a new home.

You'd think that he would be easy to sell to a beginner rider who wanted a quiet gelding to learn on, but even though several such buyers came and tried him out, none bonded with his lacklustre, head-hanging you-do-not-exist,

I-do-not-exist approach to life. No one cared to buy him. My intentions had been to pick the perfect new owner for him, perhaps a woman who would love him enough to bring him out of his shell. But winter was fast approaching, and so were the last horse sales of the year. Since I had to buy all my feed, horses that were trained had to go. I kept him until the very last, then hauled him to the local horse sale.

I felt such sadness, I almost hauled him home again. Perhaps I just hadn't tried hard enough to change what was wrong with him. I didn't know who bought him, and I didn't want to know.

The next spring I got a phone call from another horse-man who just wanted to chat about his new colts on the ground. We traded stories back and forth, surprised we hadn't run into each other at any sales last year. But wait, he had seen me ride a sorrel gelding through the ring late last year — the one with a big ugly brand on his hip. Yup, he bet that horse was a real dud. That brand belonged to someone who had destroyed the minds of more than one poor horse in his possession. It had been said, that some never did recover from his inhumane training practices. I hung up the phone shortly afterwards.

My heart had almost stopped on me. I had forgotten about Prince's brand. Now I knew. I knew who that brand belonged to; Prince's soul was laid bare for me to finally see.

This man never beat his horses. No sir, hardly ever had to use a whip or spurs on them. His claim to fame was that he could make a dude string horse out of anything. Yup, those horses towed the line when he threw those dude riders from the city up on them. The horses didn't dare blink, or they were in trouble.

What he did was the cruelest thing imaginable. If a horse acted up when he was training them to saddle, he simply roped its front feet out from under it, tied all four legs together and left it to lie in the hot, scorching sun. Hell, sometimes all night too, if he felt like it. Then afterwards, he kicked the horse until it struggled to its feet, saddled it up, and rode it all day long without food, water, or rest. He swore he rarely had to do it more than once before the horse never did a thing wrong again in its life.

I knew in my heart now, that Prince was one of those horses. I knew this man had done it more than once to what must at first have been a proud, young gelding. My mind now spoke to Prince, as if he stood before me. "How many times did it take until you finally struggled up with half paralyzed limbs to go all day with nothing to slake your thirst or ease your biting hunger, or a chance to rest your weary heart? Until you gave up entirely?"

It was then that I finally cried for Prince. I cried and screamed a silent scream for a sorrel gelding whose very soul had been snuffed from him at the hands of this man. Oh, Prince, you are gone now, but never forgotten.

Chapter 5
What Are Friends For?

hen you live alone while scratching out a living breeding, training, buying and selling horses like I do, you need support from friends and family, and I thank the good Lord daily for these people in my life. Without them, I would be toast. Trouble is, some of them will tell you that they were almost toasted themselves helping me.

Simone and the Six Pack

Take Simone for instance. A lady from town who always dresses to the Nines. It took a couple of years to get her to leave her fancy duds at home and wear good old farm clothes. For Simone these farm clothes were usually a tank top, shorts, and cute high-heeled city slicker boots. While I was protected from the elements and the horses themselves in blue jeans, long-sleeved shirts, western hat, and sturdy riding boots, she had to develop other ways to protect herself. Sun tanning lotion on one half of her body and bug repellent spray on the other half seemed to do the trick. While my boots protected me from getting a squashed toe from some horse stepping on my foot, Simone relied on her agility learned from many years of dancing to keep her toes safe. If I had to run to or from a horse in the event of a wreck happening, I thundered along as best I could. She skipped gleefully from one event to another.

Simone is French, and while I don't understand a single word of her native tongue, it didn't take long before my horses were all bilingual, which meant they worked better in two languages for her than they did in one for me.

Simone's pride and joy was the cutest little puddle-jumper of a car — white with multi-coloured decals on its sides. We nicknamed it Spot. My pride and joy was my 1450-pound stallion, Three Kits, who stood 16 hands high. His nickname was Skiddor. Skiddor grazed the lawn during summer so that he did not have to be in his paddock all the time. I failed to warn Simone that horses love to drag their teeth down the hoods of vehicles — some sort of addiction to paint, I believe. The day Skiddor left giant teeth marks all over Spot's hood, roof, and trunk, I did pick up a few choice French words.

Then there was the day I tried to get Simone killed, hand breeding a customer's snotty mare to Skiddor. This mare had a nasty temper at the best of times and was pure hell-on-four-legs once she came into heat. She was also a serious and crazed halter puller if tied to a post, so you can see why no other stallion owner had ever successfully got her bred.

I didn't want to breed this mare because of her disposition, but I failed in my feeble attempts to dissuade the owners. I demanded a complete vet check, hoping a reproductive problem would prove her unfit to carry a foal, but everything was fine. I stalled, saying I didn't want this kind of disposition passed on to one of my stallion's foals, in case he got the blame. Fine, they would not register the foal then. Because of her temperament, I demanded additional money to handle her. Done, I received a cheque for the extra money. I figured that I might as well breed her and get it over with.

My breeding corral has a snubbing post in the middle of it, with an attached, 2-inch thick cotton rope tied high and short. When little Miss Cranky came into heat, we went to the snubbing post. She couldn't break the post or pull it out of the ground. She couldn't break the rope or the heavy-duty halter I had on her either. So she would simply throw herself and hang there. Skiddor is a patient stallion and stood dozing while I came to the realization that the angle-of-the-dangle wouldn't work for him with her in that position.

Okay, so tying her up wasn't the answer. Skiddor agreed.

What Are Friends For?

I put him back out on the lawn, turned the mare loose and headed for town. On the way, I picked up Simone whose car was still in the body shop for repairs to the paint work. We made a stop at the vet's for some tranquilizer. For the mare, readers, not Simone. One Labatt's Blue was all that was needed to calm her nerves.

After Little Miss Cranky was tranquilized, I scotch hobbled her left hind leg, which was still on the ground, to protect the stallion who was taught to approach, tease, then mount from that side. Skiddor stood back beside me, waiting for permission to approach his virgin bride. Simone, to the side of the mare, had one hand on the halter and one holding a twitch firmly attached to the mare's nose. We were ready for the fun to begin.

I clucked to Skiddor, permission to approach the mare. He took two steps, while Little Miss Cranky remained totally oblivious to his approach. Not taking any chances, he gently stuck his nose out and nudged her in the flank. There was not even a blink from that mare. Growing bolder, Skiddor blew hard through his nostrils under her flank. One of her ears did jig up and down once, but that was all. I raised my hand that held his lead rope, which was permission to now do his studly duties.

The magnificent stallion rose up into the air, his forelegs circling the mare's body in a tender display of affection. And the chicken poop hit the fan!

With a scream that would have scared off an attacking

51

cougar, Little Miss Cranky exploded. Forget the tranquilizer; forget the twitch; forget the scotch hobble; she was not about to lose her virginity without a fight. She threw her head to the left and Simone lost hold of the twitch on the mare's nose. That twitch pinged off a fence post clear across the corral. One jump and the scotch hobble, which had been placed on loose so the mare could still bear weight on that leg, was the next thing to go. Everything was a blur. Simone fell and the mare lunged over her. Skiddor, still mounted on the mare, refused to leave his intended target. He, too, went over Simone. She managed to roll her body under the fence before I stepped on her. Good thing too, since my sturdy riding boots can hurt.

Simone survived, although it took awhile to calm her down. She found the last five beers from the six pack of Labatt's Blue a great help. And Little Miss Cranky? She gave birth to a pretty chestnut colt the next spring.

Grandma's Little Helper

A charming young fellow named Travis came into my life shortly after his family suffered the devastating loss of their home to fire one Christmas. To add to their distress, the father became deathly ill for a time.

Although I barely knew the family, I invited the young mother out to my place a time or two for coffee and to give her a much-needed shoulder to lean on, should she need one. She always brought her youngest son along — a little gaffer with freckles and a hint of red in his hair. He reminded me of a spunky colt who could use a few scratches behind his ears to show him that life wasn't all bad. Although he didn't think much of me petting him or scratching behind his ears, one Friday afternoon he asked if he could spend that weekend at my place. Before I could respond, his Mom said, "Sure you can, Sweetheart." As I was busy saying "Well, I have to think on that for a minute," he was fetching his backpack from his Mom's truck and before long was firmly settled on my living room couch. He informed me that the couch was his bed from now on, but I could still sit on it if I wanted to.

His Mom headed out to work and I followed her all the way to the truck, hoping to gain some much needed information. What do I feed him? Do I have to leave water out for him 24 hours a day? And the most important one of all — is he housetrained? (I should mention here that I also raise dogs.) She just smiled and told me I would do fine. How can I do fine? I don't know anything about this business of being a mother. Help!

I muttered to myself, "Okay, I can handle this," as the child followed me out to the corrals. I explained to Travis that he is not allowed in the corrals because some of these horses are rank. They are only at my place to be halter broke, a couple of weeks riding put on them or just plain gentled down a bit. Travis sighed and gently informed me that they have horses too, you know. He is not exactly a greenhorn.

By the time I walked around to the gate, he had slipped

through the rails and crawled in with Gypsy, Bell, and Tiffany. These horses were mature mares that didn't like being handled. Gypsy would take a chunk out of you with her teeth, Bell would run you over, and Tiffany would strike or kick you just for the fun of it.

"Stay calm, Gayle, stay calm," I told myself. "Don't frighten the boy or the mares." Then I screamed, "What in tarnation do you think you're doing? Don't you listen to a thing you're told? Get out of there! You're going to get yourself killed!" Travis calmly petted each mare in turn, his voice soft and loving, and they gathered around him like fleas to a dog.

The first weekend he stayed with me, I fretted so much I lost 10 pounds. By the time summer rolled around, I had grey hair and it was thinner on top from me pulling it out. While he grew and thrived out in those horse corrals, I became a nail-biting wreck. Summer meant two months of school holidays and you can guess where he decided to spend those two months. Yup, I was never going to get to sit on that couch in the evenings anymore. At least he was easy to cook for, got his own water, and was housetrained.

Then came the day he looked at me with love in his eyes and asked, "Can I call you Grandma?" Well I was prouder than an old barren mare getting a chance to be related to an awesome weanling colt. So of course I said, "Sure boy, but there ain't going to be no lazy grandsons on this spread. Now, get out there and get them yearlings caught and tied up to be dewormed."

With the patience of a saint, he replied, "They've been tied up for an hour already, Grandma. I did it while you were putting the stallion back in his pen. I also filled in your daily breeding record book for you, while you were talking to that horse buyer on the phone. Then I counted the tubes of wormer for the horses. You're short one for the yearlings, but don't worry, I checked and you did the bay filly just last month so she's okay until we get to town and buy some more. And by the way, Grandma, I checked and wormer is cheaper at the other store this month, so we can save some money by shopping there."

I just snorted, not ready to admit he sure enough was turning out to be a handy kind of boy to have around. With time, the hair might even grow back on the top of my head the way things were going. Never one to admit it, but I was sort of lonely when his parents wanted him home once in awhile in their big, new house.

Travis and I could get in more trouble than a cat cornered by a pack of dogs. One time we were pulling a horse trailer through the centre of Edmonton. I was nervous to begin with, according to my directions, I wasn't even supposed to be in Edmonton. Travis decided that if I quickly turned left at the next intersection, we could pull into that fast food restaurant to fuel ourselves up while we looked at a map. By then he had me pretty much trained to listen to his directions, so I turned left. I soon figured out that all those cars coming at me honking their horns meant I was going the wrong way on a one-way street. Travis informed me in a nice way, that we missed the restaurant, and when he turns 16, I had better let him drive.

Another time, we hauled two horses to the local horse sale. I was selling a real nice, quiet, registered, two-year-old gelding. He was selling a hammer-headed, crooked-legged, pot-bellied, totally hyped-up, brain-dead yearling gelding that his "loving" grandma gave him. My gelding was a sweetheart in the sale ring. His pride and joy went ballistic in the sale ring. His sold for twice as much as mine. Even the crowd loved this boy.

When Travis and I hauled square bales in my old pick-me-up truck, I figured a good load for the old truck was 54 bales. Travis's job was to stack on top of the load, while poor old Grandma huffed and puffed to throw the bales up to him. Then along came Mel, the man who sold me the hay. He thought my horses could sure use more bales than 54. With a grin, the strong, young man effortlessly threw another 18 bales way up there. He would have continued, but I pointed out that the truck tires were now as flat as pancakes.

He waved cheerily and left to get back to haying in another field. Travis suggested tying down the enormous load of hay perched precariously on the back of the truck. I snarled at him, "Just who is the boss here anyway? Get in the truck." At the first little bump, the entire top half of the load toppled onto the road. Travis stacked, and old Grandma threw those suckers back up to him once more. Travis calmly tied down the load of hay just like it should have been in the first place. I leaned my weary old bones against the side of the truck and wondered what I ever did before this boy came along.

Chapter 6
The Power of Love

The bond between a man or woman and a horse that loves them is a tremendous thing to witness. Love can and does heal many wounds of the soul.

I've often had to take employment in towns in order to help feed the horses and pay the bills. In one town where I was managing a hectic business, I often thought how much easier animals were to deal with than staff and customers. Nonetheless, all my staff were welcome at the farm my husband and I owned, so they could know the pleasure of being around animals. Sundays the business was closed and one wee girl in her early twenties (I'll call her Cindy), used to come out and spend time just hanging around the horses.

Others came to eat, drink, and be merry.

Cindy was a bit of a problem at work. Some days, she was jovial and put the other staff to shame with her ability to outwork them with a smile on her face. Other days, she would be sullen and quiet, seeming not to care about anything. I usually could talk the staff members into giving her a break, but customers were a different matter. I feared that I was going to have to dismiss her, yet I knew in my heart that she would be devastated at being fired. Cindy, I felt, just needed someone to help her along the often uphill path of life.

Slowly her story unfolded, while sitting around the fire-pit in the growing darkness of a summer's evening.

Raised in a hectic home, she was a forgotten item, treated like nothing more than a mistake that happened. No wonder she suffered from low self esteem. As soon as possible, she quit high school and ventured out into an often cruel world. There she met a countryman who introduced her to horses and the power of love. She was happy and content. With horses, she found a shared bond of need and trust. She learned how to handle and care for these four-legged friends. Then came the news. Her man had grown tired of her. She was shattered. As she told us this story, Cindy's sobs brought tears to my husband's eyes as well as my own.

Then began her life of drinking and mind-destroying drugs. This was the girl who now worked for me. Some days she could cope with life; many days she could not.

Out in my corrals stood a wreck of a yearling. I had

bought a bred mare to add to my broodmare band, and she foaled a grade colt, as homely as sin with twisted front legs. I had yet to sell him, even though I knew he was only good for slaughter. No one was going to buy this wreck of a colt. I trimmed his feet religiously, trying to straighten his front legs. I paid to geld him. I hoped he would grow into a head that was two sizes too big for the rest of his body. But that was never going to happen.

It was this horse Cindy was drawn to. They formed a special bond. He romped with her as if she was another colt his own age. They spun circles and frolicked together; they played games of tag. I had never bothered to name him, so she promptly named him Jumper even though with his deformed front legs he couldn't jump a mud puddle.

Finally, the time came when I had to sit her down in my office and explain that even though I thought the world of her, I was going to have to dismiss her because of her moodiness and complaints from customers and other staff members. I recommended she get counselling for the issues that were troubling her. I also recommended that she look into a different career that would allow her to work with animals, as I felt she had a natural ability to care for them. This was not easy for me, and we both ended up crying. When she stood to leave my office, she said in a small, timid, yet clear voice, "Don't sell Jumper; I'll be back to buy him." She walked out. I sniffled. Then I straightened in my chair, once again the Boss Lady I was paid to be.

Jumper wasn't any better looking as a two year old. Both his front legs still toed out so badly, he was unfit for anything except perhaps being trail ridden in a straight line. I didn't even take the time to start him under saddle. Yet, I still hadn't hauled him to an auction mart to watch him go for meat either.

Then, one day Cindy phoned me at work. She apologized for bothering me, but did I still have Jumper? She was trying her best to get her life back on track. In fact, her grandma was paying for a therapist to help her deal with her problems. She was working again but part-time, as she still had a lot of problems relating to other people. She was now renting a home in the country with a couple of other young people. Together they had several dogs, cats, and even some chickens. They had good pasture for a horse. The therapist agreed that if she loved horses, she should look into getting one. In fact he thought her heart would heal far more quickly with something of her own to love and care for. How much did I want for Jumper?

I listened quietly as she continued. She was off drugs and rarely went to a bar anymore. She was growing up. She still had a long road ahead of her, and she knew that, but perhaps Jumper would help her along the way. She remembered clearly every second she had spent with him. She had even found someone to help her train him. She felt sure that together she and Jumper could conquer the world.

I gave her Jumper. No money changed hands. I

delivered him to her place and watched her face light up with such radiance, when he stepped out of the trailer.

The rest is a fairy tale come true. Cindy told me that it was Jumper who finally broke through the ties binding her heart. He gave her unconditional love and never judged her when she made mistakes. When she needed a friend to talk to, Jumper listened, often deep into the night, rubbing his head on her chest while her arms were wrapped around his neck. Even as I write this, Cindy still owns Jumper. He is very old now and arthritis has affected his front legs, but the pair of them still go for short trail rides now and then on his 'feeling good' days.

The crooked legged horse that I almost sold for meat so very many years ago will draw his last breath on her and her family's land when the time is right. Cindy, her husband, and children will mourn his passing.

Chapter 7

The Mare Who Got into the Whisky Barrel

I n the olden days, I had a four-year-old, first-time foaling mare. She foaled with one mighty small udder for such a big, well-fed mare. Sure, the filly was getting some much-needed colostrum, but nowhere near enough milk to survive. By eight hours old, she had resorted to sucking the few drops of milk from her dam, then burying her tiny muzzle in the water tank and gulping down water. Desperate, I phoned the old-time vet who was the only one in the area. He didn't know of any shots at that time to give a mare to increase her milk supply. But he did have the oddest thing for me to try. He claimed it would work within hours.

He told me to phone the nearest distillery that made whisky. Apparently, after the whisky is siphoned off for us to guzzle, a sludge is left in the bottom of the wooden barrel. The distilleries dry the sludge into a powder which is used for medicinal purposes (just animals I hope) and for fertilizer to grow super-sized plants. (I have no idea if these super-sized plants lean slightly to the side or sway even when there is no breeze.)

I ordered a 5-pound bag of this dried whisky mash, which they put on the midnight express bus to my town. When I went to the bus terminal to pick it up, the lady handed me the package with her nose all wrinkled up. It wasn't my horsy smell bothering her, but the smell coming from inside the brown paper wrapping. It was so bad, I transported it home in the back of the truck, not inside the cab with me.

I mixed a hefty dose of the powder in the mare's morning grain. She took to the taste of it like an old drunk who's been deprived for quite a spell. She had another feeding in the afternoon, then again at night. By the next morning's feeding that mare was hooked on the stuff. She wasn't leaning sideways or tripping over her own feet, but I swear she had a glazed look in her eyes. By nighttime, she was milking like a Holstein cow, and the little filly was in seventh heaven.

Strange as it was, this old-time remedy worked. The filly couldn't consume all that available milk, and the mare eventually got over her need for her three-times-a-day fix of leftover whisky.

Chapter 8
Stormy's Donkeys

This book on horses would not be complete without a tale about the charming donkey, relative to the horse. My dear friend, Stormy O'Shea, an avid donkey fan who keeps some of the little critters around just for amusement sake, has had some fun times with her donks. Here's what she has to say.

All the books say a donkey is just like a horse. They are part of the equine family. Whoever wrote those words of wisdom should have interviewed my small herd of donkeys. They would have brayed stridently that they certainly were not just like a horse, although they do share some similarities. They all have the basic body shape, except for those beautiful long ears on the donks. They eat hay and oats, and graze on lush grass. Most have a love of carrots, apples, and specially made horse treats. However, being owned by several donkeys, I know they are miles apart from horses.

You can put most horses in a corral and not worry too much about them being bored. Put several more in, and they will usually stand around waiting patiently to be fed or let out. Not so with donks. They will constantly circle the pen, looking for anything to snack on, nibble at, chew to bits, or push out of shape.

Donkey Games

I was in my garden one afternoon, when a pickup came flying up the driveway. Two rugged cowboys spilled out whooping with laughter. I called out a greeting but all they could do was point out to the pasture, tears of laughter streaming down their cheeks. I knew immediately that my donks were up to something. Sure enough, they were.

Two of them had found an old white feed sack. With their teeth firmly clamped one on each end they were racing madly in a circle, much like two children holding hands and spinning. As we watched, one let go and the other galloped towards a group of young colts sharing the corral. The donkey whacked them with wild enthusiasm on their rear ends with the sack. The poor colts stampeded from pillar to post, with the donk in hot pursuit.

Meanwhile, my husband had come out of the barn to see who had driven up. When he saw the donkeys' antics, he shot me a look that told me I was in big trouble. Not that it worried me much. It was nothing that a juicy steak dinner followed by a thick slice of apple pie couldn't fix. Of course, he wanted me to tell the cowboys what had happened the day before and how one of those darn long eared critters almost caused two old ladies to have heart attacks.

Abby's Cat

Abby is a donkey I rescued, and she had grown into a beauty. I learned early she needed toys to amuse herself. Since I have a bevy of tiny housedogs, I keep a huge box of stuffed animals for them to play with. I chose a realistic looking orange cat that was too big for the small dogs to play with. Out to Abby it went. She was delighted! She immediately grabbed the stuffed thing by the tail, then lit out at full gallop for the pasture. Donkeys are generous, so they like to share new toys. The colts saw her coming and didn't appreciate Abby's enthusiasm. They galloped full steam out to the back forty.

Having no other playmates, she amused herself by swinging the cat by the tail, whipping it in a circle, then letting it fly into the air in a high arc. Once it landed, she would trot over to it, stomp on it a few times, pick it up by the tail and do it all over again. I was bent over double, laughing at her antics, when a car screeched to a stop in the driveway.

Two little grey-haired ladies tumbled out in a dither. "What kind of person are you to allow a donkey to hurt that poor cat? And you're standing here doing nothing?" One lady had a cane, which she pounded on the ground with every word. The yelling continued. "We're going to report you. Just see if we don't. Get out there and rescue that poor cat. It's probably dead! If that sad, mangled thing is still alive, we'll take it straight to the vet."

As I tried to explain, their shrieking drowned me out. Meanwhile Abby was trying something new. She had the cat by the head and was methodically banging it against a fence post. The old ladies were in hysterics by now, jumping up and down in a rage. I wondered if I should offer to make them a nice pot of calming tea.

All the racket caught Abby's attention. Still with the stuffed cat dangling from her teeth, she trotted up to the fence. She dropped the toy and put one foot on it. By this time, the dear ladies were hanging on to each other moaning and sobbing. Abby liked the sound. She sucked in some wind and roared out one good bray after another.

With every bray, the women seemed to shrink in size. I finally reached under the fence and yanked the stuffed cat out, showing them it was just a toy. Not a real cat. I thought they would be relieved and would smile and then apologize for all the nasty things they had said.

Not so. In perfect unison they screeched, "You are sick, sick, sick! What sort of person gives a donkey a thing like that to play with?" There was more thumping with the cane, this time on the hood of the car. Abby liked that sound too, so she continued braying. Anyone who knows donkeys understands what a loud, powerful voice they have. While Abby was enjoying her sing, the ladies who had worked themselves into a fine lather, decided they had had enough of this crazy place.

Both women tried to get into the car from the same side. One leaned on the horn. The other used her cane like a cattle prod to hurry her companion into the vehicle. Both were still hollering.

They finally stuffed themselves into the car, rolled down the windows and continued to hurl insults at me. I was impressed. I had no idea that tiny old ladies would have such a wide selection of cuss words.

I didn't give Abby back her stuffed cat. Being a little rattled by the whole scene, I dug out a large cardboard box for her to play with. When I tossed it over the fence to her, she flipped it with a foot. It flew into the air, landing on her head. She thought it was great fun! Abby trotted out to the pasture where the colts were grazing. It was too much for them to handle — a donkey, minus a head, coming right towards them.

I wonder if our colts will some day need psychiatric help for the trauma my donkeys have inflicted on them. More likely they will turn out able to handle anything. As for me, I look forward to each day wondering what new thing my donkeys will come up with, knowing they'll serve up a lot of laughter as good old stress relief.

Chapter 9
A Case of the Strangles

L ife is not always a bed of roses when you're raising horses. There are good times and there are bad. You learn to cope with the challenges anyway you can, and you learn to depend on the veterinarians in your life. Without them, many a horse would be lost.

I had purchased a pretty, grey yearling filly sight unseen and had her delivered to my home. She looked to be in good health when unloaded from the trailer, but I put her in a separate pen away from the others as a safety precaution. The next day she wasn't looking very chipper, and sure enough, she was in the first stage of distemper (strangles), a highly contagious equine disease. And separate pen or not, all my other horses started to get strangles, too.

I have long followed the advice to let strangles run its course unless the animal is desperately ill with it, and none of my horses were so sick that they needed treatment. They were an unhappy bunch with their swollen glands under the jaw, but the glands were draining without assistance.

Only my 20-year-old mare, Lady, showed no signs of having contracted the disease. When I did a final check on the horses just before dark, I found Lady far from the herd, sitting like a dog. She was in terrible distress and the ground around her was torn up from her struggling. Finding a horse in this unnatural position is a desperate situation. I phoned the closest vet to come right away. He diagnosed her quickly. His diagnosis was that she had colicked and had a twisted gut or ruptured bowel. He advised she should be destroyed immediately, as she could not survive this condition.

I was well aware that horses found in this unnatural position usually had a twisted gut or ruptured bowel, but I suggested that she instead might have bastard strangles (when the disease moves from the head to the internal cavity) and that the pain was causing her to adopt the position she was in. The vet repeated his diagnosis and offered to destroy the mare for me or I could shoot her myself. He had no intention of trying to treat a horse already dead on its feet. He is not an unkind man, but he did not want to stand by and watch her suffer.

Old Lady did not deserve to suffer, but she did deserve

further examination before pulling the trigger. I asked the vet to give her a high dose of painkiller and another dose for me to give to her later on the long trip to the university in Saskatoon, the only facility that might be able to save her. He grudgingly agreed. Within minutes, the pain was masked by the drug and she was able to stand. Still, her heart rate was far too high for her to keep going much longer. I loaded her in the trailer and set off down the long, lonely highway.

I cannot say enough about the veterinarian staff at the University of Saskatchewan. After arriving, they quickly confirmed a serious case of bastard strangles. They agreed to try to save her, but did not hold out much hope.

The first task was to get her pulse back down to an acceptable level, and they gave themselves only a couple of hours to do so. They succeeded. It was a lengthy, uphill battle for her life over the next several days. She was kept drugged so she was free of pain. The vets were repeatedly forced to tap into her under-belly, to drain off the pus accumulating inside her. She was administered gallons of fluids by intravenous drip into her jugular, 24 hours a day.

For days they never left her stall, drawing on all their knowledge to save the life of this grand old mare. And she did survive. In fact, although heavily pregnant during this ordeal, miraculously she didn't lose the foal. His name is Zeke and he is a beauty to behold. Had I not insisted on a second opinion so long ago, two horses would have died that day, not just one.

Chapter 10
Cow Tales

Everyone thinks that being a cowgirl out on the open range must be so much fun. And it is, if you like long days, seven days a week. The job has its perks. You get to ride with all those good-looking cowboys, for a start. And if they are the Real McCoy, they even like you with calf manure smeared on your cheeks and sweat stains in the armpits of your shirt. As long as you can hold up your end of the job, they may even give you the occasional compliment. "Hey Blondie, get that nag of yours in high gear or I may have to come over there and slap your little rump."

You say to yourself, "I love this guy already; he thinks my rump is little."

"Hey Blondie, nice job of cutting that lame steer out of the herd. One of these days I'm going to take you to town and buy you a beer." You turn beet red, after all, didn't he just ask you out on a date in cowboy lingo?

"Hey Blondie, I sure hope you can cook as good as you can ride." Oh, my Gawd! I barely know this dude and he wants to marry me. Why else is he wondering if I can cook? I am going to go straight to town to buy some cook books. It's time I learned how to make something besides chili and beans anyway.

Now there is a difference between a real cowgirl working on a big ranch and one who rides horses for pleasure. You know the ones I mean, with the jeans so tight they must be painted on. In the real world, when you are riding horses 10 to 14 hours a day, you don't wear skin-tight jeans. You wear comfortable jeans, so you can get up and down off that horse countless times a day, chase that calf on foot, wrestle bare-handed with the calf's irate mother, and then give a shot of penicillin to that 2000-pound bull with foot rot. You wear pants you can actually run in if you have to.

A Snotty Cow

I was glad I was wearing my comfortable jeans the time I got day work from a rancher helping round up some stray cows on a large grazing lease. It was mostly dense bush, with occasional cattle or game trails and uncooperative cows. We had spilt up, gone to the far reaches of the land and were now pushing strays towards a holding area on the flats along the river.

The strays were small groups of cow/calf pairs that were content living right where they were. None seemed overly enthusiastic about being moved home for the fall and winter.

I was quite happy with the few I had convinced to mosey along, staying well back of them to keep them calm, so they wouldn't get riled up and head in the wrong direction.

Then I spotted a lone Angus cow off to my right. She was standing motionless back in the tree line — head up, watching me but obviously thinking she was hidden. I always had to chuckle over these critters who had grown wild enough during a summer in the high country to think that they now blended into the bush like a deer. Since she was as black as the ace of spades, she didn't blend in at all.

I eased my gelding back, meaning to circle in behind the cow and get her headed out. The trouble is that when I approached her, she did not mosey off in the right direction but instead spun to face me, with her head up in the air. She shook her head, warning me she wasn't interested in cooperating. A quick glance told me she was a dry cow who had lost her calf a long time ago. The good news was that I didn't have to hunt for the calf. The bad news was that sometimes these old single cows with no calf can be harder to convince to join the others.

I slapped my hand on my chaps and hollered for her to move out. She took two steps in my direction, shook her head again and pawed the ground with a front foot, throwing dirt up on her back.

Great. Why did I have to be the one to find some old snotty cow? I hollered again, slapping my leg for more sound effects and jumped my gelding towards her. These three things combined should have worked, and I should have been looking at her back end going away from me. Instead, she lowered her head to the attack position, threw more dirt up on her back and gave me an ear splitting bellow, which in cow language meant "attack mode now on standby."

I hollered again. She bellowed again, and a split second later she charged my horse. She rooted him a good swipe on the left shoulder before I got him turned around in the heavy bush to get out of her way. She then gave him a parting thump in the rear end as we were leaving.

The gelding took everything in stride as if getting hit by a cow was something that happened all the time and was no big deal. I made a mental note to jack the price up on him a bit for having more than his fair share of common sense.

I circled the cow again, making lots of noise in the bush, trying to get her to leave the country. She circled with me, head lowered, ready to fight. So I moved in close, then spun the gelding around, looking back over my shoulder to check that she was hot on his tail. Sure enough, she chased us a good 50 yards, before taking another stand. And that is how I got her down to the bunched cattle along the river. Stop, go back and bug her, have her chase us several yards. Stop and do it over again.

Several men were lounging around the holding area watching this performance once we hit the open pasture. I realized my method of chasing cows would seem odd to these cowboys. I also realized that since I was the only woman on the roundup, I was likely in for a bit of ribbing. I figured the one I had secretly nicknamed "Backscratcher" due to his three day growth of prickly stubble on his chin would be the worst heckler. Or perhaps "Drugstore Cowboy," the one with the expensive cowboy boots, silver spurs, and bright red bandana tied around his neck. Or maybe it would be "Weasel," the small one with the shifty eyes and quick, jerky movements that even bothered his horse. I prayed that "Handsome Man," the good-looking charmer my age would not be the one to rib me, since I kind of liked the way he filled out his blue jeans. I was secretly hoping to impress him with what a great cowgirl I was.

Dismounting from my horse, I stretched and busied myself with loosening my cinch. Ignoring the men gathered around me, I rubbed my horse's shoulder, letting him know I was pleased with his performance. Much to my chagrin, Handsome Man just couldn't help himself, "You're sort of new at this chasing cows business, aren't you?" he said. "Perhaps I should explain to you that you chase cows from behind them, not in front of them." At this, the rest of the men exploded in loud guffaws, thinking Handsome Man was the smartest thing since sliced bread.

Slowly I turned towards my tormentor, trying to think of

an appropriate and lady-like comeback. I was prepared to bat my eyelashes if necessary. But I didn't have to because just then I noticed that he had tiny hairs growing out of his nostrils and I just don't like a man sporting nose hair, no matter how he fills out his blue jeans!

Scared Stiff

Not all horses stay calm and controllable after getting kicked by a cow. In fact, over the years I learnt that some react in a completely unpredictable way.

I did a fair amount of riding on a neighbour's ranch since I lived on a small acreage. In return for letting me mile out horses on his land, I kept an eye on his cattle for him. Most of his bottomland was cleared and planted to pasture, but there was plenty of bush and timber remaining higher up the slopes. It was a pleasant place to ride.

I had several weeks' riding on a three-year-old gelding and although he had a bit of spook in him, he was a nice horse. While trotting down a cut line on him, I came across a mother cow in the bush. I could see her calf lying on the ground beside her. The calf was not lying up on his chest in a healthy position, but flat on the ground, head thrown back. From the position he was in, I figured him to be dead and past any help from me. But unless I got close enough to see if he was breathing or not, I couldn't know for sure.

I moved quietly towards the cow, so she wouldn't think she had to get into 'protect my calf' mode. I circled her, coming in even closer, but still I could not figure out if the calf was breathing. The cow shook her head at me, blowing drops from her nose. I sure didn't want to tangle with an irate mother cow, but I still couldn't see the calf well enough. Now, any old cowman will tell you, "Keep the calf between you and the cow to prevent getting hit." I followed this advice and eased the already tense gelding towards the calf, with Momma on guard duty on the other side of it.

At about the same time that I saw that the calf was indeed no longer in the world of the living, Momma cow decided to put the run on me. She dropped her head and charged. I was too close to get out of her way in the thicket of small trees. She hooked my horse in the cinch area, and I got ready for the wreck to happen. This green-broke gelding was about to blow, and I just hoped I could stay with him.

Instead, he froze. She hooked him under the belly again, just missing my leg by inches. She then hammered him in the hind leg. The silly horse just took the beating, making no attempt to get away. Frantic, I spanked his butt with the reins, and I swear he rooted himself more firmly to the spot.

The old cow made one more pass at him then turned tail. She had made her final stand to protect her dead offspring.

I knew I was in bigger trouble now than if the horse had blown up and taken off running and bucking. He was trembling violently and his mind was shot. He wasn't able to rationalize what had just happened or to figure out that the danger was over. He had me plumb spooked, because I knew I didn't want to be anywhere near him, let alone on him, when he finally decided to move.

I stepped off him slowly and gently, and inched as far from him as I could while still holding onto the reins. I moved towards his rear and pulled on the rein to untrack him and get him to move.

He moved all right. He shot straight in the air, came down, reared and flipped right over backwards. He lunged back to his feet and then his ears started to rotate — a positive sign that he was able to think again.

I had let go of the reins when he came unglued. Talking quietly to him, I picked up his reins again. I pulled on his head again, and he followed the pull without exploding. I led him around a bit, until he was almost back to normal. He was not seriously injured physically, so I approached him to mount. The old cow had hammered him on his left side. I reached towards the stirrup and he started to kick. He just stood there and kicked with that hind leg. Wham, wham, wham. Okay, I would just have to mount him from the right side. I moved around to that side, reached for the stirrup and he switched kickers just as quick. He didn't do anything else; he just stood there and kicked.

I headed for home, leading him. Every once in awhile he would kick straight out behind. After about a mile, I was able to mount in between the now sporadic kicks.

He kicked on and off all the way home. I turned him out

for a couple of weeks, and he was fine after that. But I sure didn't check cows on him again.

Chapter 11
Old Flip

I love listening to my 82-year-old mother, Becky Caskey, tell stories about when she was a young girl. Born in Alberta in 1921, she grew up when horses worked the land and pulled the buggies to town. Granddad and his brother grew tall, yellow crops of grain, raised some of the best purebred horned Hereford cattle, and never lacked for horse power.

Their teams came in all sizes, ages, and colours. In those days, horses were not pets; they worked for their hay and oats. They were well cared for, but until age brought them down, they leaned into their collars, straining to haul their loads. And the horses loved it. Many a horse was disgusted to be left behind when the workday began at morning light, and showed it by nickering and dancing to go too. They were bred to work, and the best of them are fondly remembered to this day.

Mom has told me many amusing and touching stories of the special horses in her life — Blazer, Beauty, Star Lion, Judy, and a team of bay Hamiltonians named Buster and Barney.

Mom raised the orphan colt, Blazer, by hand. The colt still loved drinking milk from an old mixing bowl even when he was two years old. He would paw at an old log outside the house to summon mother for his milk. He pawed a hole almost right through the log before finally giving up his addiction.

Mom brought another favourite horse of hers, named Beauty, into the house porch one time just to see if she could. Grandma tried chasing them out by whacking them both with a straw broom. Poor Mom was squashed against the porch wall by the panicked horse trying to turn around in the confined space to get away from that broom.

Mom also tells the tragic story of Uncle's favourite mare, called Judy, who shared a soul-deep bond with him. One day she tripped in a badger hole. Uncle was thrown and broke his leg. A neighbour saw the horse standing there and went to investigate. Judy refused to let this stranger near her fallen rider, whirling around Uncle in protective anger to keep the man away. He was forced to walk a long way to fetch Granddad. Then came the sad day Judy refused to leave the corral when asked to. Uncle picked up a small stone and winged it at her to get her to move. Such a tiny stone, but it struck her on the front leg, shattering the bone.

Uncle in his grief and despair, had to shoot his beloved mare. He skinned her, tanned the hide and slept with this horsehide blanket for the rest of his life. I now own this blanket. Although it is well over 70 years old, it remains one of my most prized possessions.

But there is one horse from my mother's past that stands out above all the rest — Old Flip.

Flip was raised in the Oyen, Alberta area. While still a wee foal, her mother was put to work doing road construction. Running beside her sweating mother, Flip soon became quick and agile, as she leapt aside out of harm's way, hurdled over banks of dirt, and turned on a dime to avoid collisions with men and other teams bent to the task at hand.

One day when she was older, a neighbour's big breeding bull escaped from its pasture. Three horsemen were summoned to get him back in. Soon the bull was plumb riled up and in a murderous temper. It hooked the underbelly of one of the horses, tossing the horse and its rider over backwards. Flip, being ridden by another man, proved her quickness and ability to handle the snorty old bull. She whirled in behind the bull and bit his rump, sinking her teeth into him again and again. The bull was fast and kept whirling to hook her. But Flip was faster, spinning around and around with him, with her snapping jaws repeatedly finding their target.

Finally the defeated bull headed for his home range. He had had enough of the demon horse.

Flip was built much like today's popular breed of horse — the quarter horse. She could turn on a dime and give you a nickel in change. When you said, "Whoa," she stopped dead in her tracks, and you better be prepared for it or be flung over her head.

Mom was almost eight years old, when Uncle bought Flip. She stood in awe as he led her up the lane. Wow, her very own school horse. She was a sharp-looking bay mare with a squiggly white blaze on her forehead. They became friends right away. Flip trusted Mom, and Mom loved her. They were meant for each other.

Flip was head shy and hated anyone touching her face. It wasn't clear what her second owner, an often cruel horse-man, had done to her. What Mom did know was that her tongue had been almost cut in half. A deep scarred groove remained. Flip was a confirmed halter puller, freaking out if tied by the halter on her head. She would pull and fight being tied until every single rope broke. What was Mom going to do? Well, she tied her up by her front foot, which Flip never minded in the least. Granddad put a small leather strap with a buckle onto a short piece of rope for Mom. Flip would lift her foot up, so Mom could buckle it around her pastern, then stand patiently while tied up at home, at the school house, church, or anywhere.

Mom didn't ride Flip often. She couldn't stay on a horse

and no one could figure out why. After all, her brother had been riding since he was five years old. He was an excellent rider. Mom simply fell off every time she got on a horse; that was all there was to it. She loved horses and had no fear of them whatsoever, but falling onto hard ground again and again was no fun. Instead, she hitched Flip to a buggy and went to school that way. She never had to pick up the shafts of the buggy for Flip; Flip would just back straight in for her. But if anyone else tried to do it, Flip would back crooked and straddle first one shaft, then the other.

The buggy worked wonders for her, until winter set in. Now what were Granddad and Uncle going to do so she could make the 14-mile round trip, to school? They did not own a cutter for a single horse. This was the late 1920s, a time of little money but great pioneer spirit and resourcefulness. A homemade toboggan was fashioned from an old binder platform. Mom's brother made a hood for it like the one found on a baby's buggy. Shafts for Flip were added, and Mom's very own "bumperett" was born. It didn't have a seat in it, so Mom sat on a tanned sheepskin on the floor. Heavy rugs kept her warm. As time went on, the bottom of the bumperett began to wear thin so runners were attached to the base. This was Mom's winter conveyance for all of her school years.

Flip did not like other horses to pass her. One cold winter morning on the way to school, Flip had broken trail through the deep fresh snow, when someone with a team decided to pass them. She was pretty upset about that. Then a boy on a young black mare galloped past. This was just too much of an insult for Flip. She decided to gallop also. Going around a bend in the road, the bumperett ticked her heels, and she was off like a shot. First, she passed the team like they were standing still. Then she shot past that boy on the galloping mare, showing him how fast a real racehorse could run. This was a lot of fun, until Mom realized they were completely out of control and headed straight towards the school's barn doors. She thought a terrible wreck was about to happen, but Flip came to a screeching halt just in time. Unfortunately, when they came to a standstill, the bumperett was perched on top of a snow bank and Flip was below on the path, which made it a challenge to unhitch her.

The last winter that Mom went to the little white schoolhouse on the prairies, the temperature hovered around –37° Celsius all of January and right into February. The blizzards started most afternoons. Grandpa had always told her that if she was caught in a blizzard, to let the horse go where it wanted to. A horse's sense of direction is far better than a human's.

Well let me tell you, the first thing that happens in a blizzard is that your trail vanishes under drifting, blowing snow. In the whiteout, Flip and Mom got to the last long hill, and then lost the trail. Mom remembered what Grandpa had told her and gave Flip her head, trusting her to get them home safely. Flip ploughed ahead, her face bent into the wind. After what seemed like forever, she came to a halt. No matter how Mom urged her to get going again, she refused to move. When Mom got out and walked around in front of Flip to investigate, she found flimsy square boards sticking up out of a snow bank. Now she knew where they were! She and Flip had drifted to the southeast of the yard, and those boards were part of the roof of the root cellar that Grandpa had dug into the side of a sandy hill. Below those flimsy boards was a deep pit. Had Flip taken another step, they would have crashed through and perished. They never would have been found in blizzard conditions so far off the trail.

Growing up on a lonely prairie farm, Mom had no one to tell all her worldly troubles to. No one but Flip. Many a time, when Mom was sad about something and needed a friend, she would talk to Flip. Flip would nudge her with her nose, then she would lay her old head on Mom's shoulder and close her eyes. They would stand like that, a girl and her horse.

There was not a lot of feed in the Dirty Thirties and Forties, and farmers struggled just to feed their cattle. In winter, all horses were turned out on the prairie to paw for feed off the land. Only a team and one good saddle horse were kept in the barn for the winter months. When Flip was 32 years old, Mom begged her dad to let the old mare stay home for the winter, but her pleas fell on deaf ears. Feed was just too precious.

Flip managed to make it home in the early spring. She was terribly thin with such sunken eyes. She walked up to the old barn doors and lay down, never to rise again. Mom felt such terrible grief. Old Flip, not just a horse, but a dear friend.

Chapter 12
Lights Out!

hrough years of raising, training, and buying and selling horses, I've learned a lot of things. I've learned that if you raise horses right, they are much easier to train than the ones you purchase from auction sales. Horses from auctions have often been spoiled rotten or they've been scared spitless by someone mishandling them. You have to work to remedy these things in order to make good horses out of them.

Buying them off the open range was a common practice of mine in the 1970s. I only had to outbid the meat horse buyers to get the majority of these wild-eyed critters. Back in those days, they were mostly grade horses of unknown pedigree, but I would only buy the good looking beggars with nice conformation. They were often not castrated, had matted manes and tails, and blew snorts of terror through their noses. Half the time they had never seen a man on foot let alone been this close to a whole pack of humans. They had never been fed hay or grain, and had grown up fighting to survive, struggling to find food or shelter. They had learned to flee from predators or to stand and fight. They were tough horses either frightened out of their wits or on the warpath, looking for a fight. I tried to pick out the in-between ones. The ones that were only going to break one or two bones, not outright kill me.

In the good old days, we seldom had round pens or arenas to ride our horses around day in and day out. Instead, we hoped for some old cow corral that was high enough and strong enough to get them halter broke and gelded. Then trainers such as myself worked with them for two or three days, by gently touching them all over with our hands, talking softly to them, earning their trust. We eased in close to lay an old saddle blanket on, over and around them. Most of us never thought of tying plastic bags or other paraphernalia onto long whips to touch them all over in order to stay back and protect ourselves. So we got struck, kicked, or bitten occasionally, but we called it "hands on" training. We never thought of chasing a horse away from us, making him go around and around, until he "joined up" with us by learning that the only place he got to rest was right beside us.

Instead, many of us trainers were proud when we could

say, "Lookie here! He just came to me to be scratched. He trusts me." "Why, the bugger likes me. Look at the way he is following me around!" We never had fancy words for it back then. Phrases such as "joining up" hadn't been invented yet. I know that the broncs came to me because they trusted me, not because the only place that was safe from being chased around a pen was beside me or following me. And I'm not talking about today's average horse that is handled since birth. I'm talking about horses that were semi-wild and real tough from life's hard lessons of survival of the fittest.

After a couple or three days of working with these horses, they were saddled and ridden out on the land, not in the safety of pens or arenas. Some took to the saddle and being ridden like they'd been doing it all their lives. I often put a lot of extra time on these nicer ones. The day I could slide off their rumps, crawl under their bellies, cross a creek or river on them, throw a rope off them, and ride them bareback, they went to good homes. The families would never have guessed their fat, fancy, and trimmed up gelding at one time shivered and shook at the sight of a human.

Some were snotty broncs, and many of them could buck without needing much excuse. A lot of cowboys didn't care though. These horses didn't cost a fortune and they added some excitement to their lives. Old-time cowboys weren't afraid of anything on four legs back then.

One tough horse I thought the world of was a grade black gelding I purchased from a stock contractor. He had been used as a bareback bronc and never did learn to like being a saddle horse. But I just had to have him, because I needed a black horse to get married on. That's a pretty good reason for this cowgirl.

I survived the wedding on him and went on to continually place in the top four in competitive trail riding. Twenty-five milers, 50 milers, Son didn't care. I gave him a job to do and he did it. All he asked was that I allow him his self-respect and didn't pet him too much or too long when the awards were handed out. He never did learn to appreciate that human/horse bonding thing, after his stint as a rodeo bronc.

When I worked high up in the Rocky Mountains for an outfitter for a couple of years, I found it was an excellent place to take these critters and put some distance on them. A couple of 10-day trips and they were as broke as most horses are in three months. They not only learned what long days were, they learned to navigate fast flowing rivers and narrow trails on the edges of cliffs. They could jump fallen logs and twist-'n-turn through heavy timber. They had to skid old trees to camp for firewood and carry a pack saddle, if need be. They learned what hobbles were made for and to not spook at wildlife. I still say to this day, no amount of arena riding could ever produce a better all around using horse.

But I never was much good at riding a bucking horse. Oh, I tried, all right, especially if someone was watching. Lordy, there is nothing in the world more embarrassing than kissing the ground with someone watching. With the first jump, I would be trying to bring that old pony's head up and around to stop him. Pretty much by the second jump, I was already looking for the perfect place to land. By the third jump I had mentally said my "Goodbye Cruel World" speech. By the fourth I was picking dirt out from between my teeth and feeling sorry for myself.

And the very worse part about being a cowgirl is you have to dust yourself off and get back on. None of this scaredy-cat stuff for us, regardless of bruised body and wounded pride. You can shed a few tears if you must, but you gotta get up, tuck your shirt back into your belt and go catch the sucker who dumped you in the dirt.

You tighten the cinch another notch, tuck his head around to have some chance and step up there. If you know any prayers, this is the time to start mumbling them in the hopes that the Higher Power up above might take pity on you.

The last time I had an unwanted instant dismount from a horse, I thought I had figured out how not to get hurt anymore in my old age.

I had pretty much quit training horses and wasn't missing it all that much. I was happy breeding a few select mares to my stallion and selling the nice colts they were putting on the ground for me. So why I let myself get talked into putting 30 days on a basically unhandled stallion, I don't know. Could it be that us old cowgirls have a hard time hanging up our spurs once and for all?

He was a pretty sorrel with excellent bloodlines and a nice way of moving. I picked him up in his owner's pasture, loading one of his mares first in the trailer to get him to cooperate and get in himself. Then I backed the mare out, closed the end gate, and headed for home. He stomped around in there quite a bit, rocking the boat to inform me I had made a mistake.

I stuck him in a corral for a couple of days to get over missing his wives and then started working with him. Once he learned that he couldn't push me around, we began to get along.

In fact, I took to liking him, as he was a quick learner. He offered little resistance to ground work so I dusted off my old bronc saddle hanging in the shed and showed it to him. He snorted at it just to blow the last of the dust off, and I saddled him up. He moseyed around the corral, unconcerned. I slipped the D-ring snaffle into his mouth and he mouthed it with no real worry. I left him to pack the equipment around while I went and fed the mares.

I don't know what set him off, but with a squeal he blew. And how he could buck! This was no half-hearted attempt; there was a whole lot of daylight showing under his belly. I was plumb happy to not only be on the ground but in the next pen over too. He was kicking high and hard. Then he just stopped in his tracks. Calmly he started wandering around the corral again, as if nothing had happened.

Just to be on the safe side, I ground drove him for the

next two days. Then I stepped up on him. He was a sweetheart if I ever rode one. He gave willingly to the bit and was soon turning and stopping like a saint. The next day he was backing a couple of steps when asked, and keeping his head in real good position. By the third day we were loping slow circles in the pen, and I was in love with his willing disposition.

Because he was a stallion, I locked all the horses away from the centre paddock the next day, when we took our first outside ride. He acted so nice, I was kind of wishing I owned him — until I dismounted to put him back into the pen to unsaddle. I barely got the pen gate open and for no reason at all, he blew. With his first jump into the pen, he was kicking holes in the sky with those back feet. Two more wicked jumps and bang, just like that he quit. He turned around and came back to me, rubbing his head on my shoulder, all apologetic for his ungentlemanly behaviour. I tightened the cinch and worked him another 10 minutes in the pen, going over what he had already learned, to try and figure out what the problem was. He was as good as gold.

Once I had him unsaddled, I checked his back for anything sore, then checked the saddle and blanket for something that might be bugging him. I couldn't find anything, so I figured something weird was going on in his head.

I have always firmly believed that the sooner you get horses out of the corrals and put some distance on them in the open, the better they are for it. Get them out and give

them something easy to do besides going around in circles —
follow a cow or two or take them down through the timber
and get them turning through the trees. So that weekend I
spent the morning teaching him to load and unload nicely
from the trailer and then loaded him up to head about
7 miles from my home. Here was the perfect training area —
six quarters of secluded, unfenced timber with lots of trails
through it.

Due to advancing age and one too many broken bones
in the past, I did something I never used to do when young.
I took a cell phone with me and phoned a friend. I told her
where I was, what I was doing, and gave her instructions to
call an ambulance if I didn't phone her within two hours,
because I was going to need one.

The sorrel was super. We covered a lot of ground and he
worked like a pro, although he was prone to whistle a shrill
stallion call once in awhile, showing me his mind wasn't entirely on the job at hand. When a gelding from a good half mile
away answered him, he pulled a real studly act for a few minutes until I got his mind back on me. Then he was good again.

For the next three days it poured rain and I was unable
to ride him. When the sun finally surfaced, we worked in the
corral for awhile, then headed for the tall timber again. I
unloaded him and phoned my friend with the same
instructions.

I laid the cell phone on the truck seat, tightened the
stallion's cinch, led him around a bit, and then stepped up.

He took a few steps, and then he blew. There was no reason for it, and no warning. He snapped me back in that saddle hard. I knew I couldn't ride him, because he had yanked all the slack out of the reins and had free access to buck uncontrolled. But I intended to give it my best shot. I had never before gone for the saddle horn on a bucking horse, but I did this time. I got a death grip on that baby and hollered at him to give it his best shot. He was hitting the ground so hard he was grunting with every jump. For a spilt second, I fancied that I was good enough to stay with him. Then I lost my grip on the saddle horn!

If you lose your grip when you're leaning back to ride those hard hitting jumps, then you're going off over the back end. I remember everything as clear as if it were yesterday. As if in slow motion, I passed over his rump, just as he was kicking high. I felt him connecting with me again while I was in midair. Then the ground came up to meet me, and it was lights out!

I know I was unconscious for about 20 minutes, because I remember looking at my watch just before I stepped up on him. I looked again when I came to. I remembered that I was to phone my friend to let her know I was okay when I got back to the parked truck and trailer. There was the truck only a few yards from me. But why was I lying on the ground? I rolled over and there was a horse, calmly grazing. Whose horse was that? And where was its owner? He must be pretty stupid to let his horse graze with the reins dragging on the ground.

I got to my feet and except for feeling kind of numb in my head and neck, I seemed okay. I figured I better catch that horse before he stepped on his reins and hurt his mouth. The horse stood quietly for me to catch it. Now what was I going to do with it? I looked around. Where was its owner? I didn't have all day to stand there holding onto a horse.

I was feeling kind of dizzy, so I decided to load the horse into my trailer until the owner showed up.

The stallion stepped up in the trailer nice and proper, just like a horse I would have taught how to load. I closed the end gate and moved weakly around to the driver's side of the truck. There lay a horse halter and lead rope. My halter and lead rope. Everything came rushing back then. I sat down hard, as my confused mind adjusted.

I decided I had better not drive. I would phone my friend and tell her to come get me, but I couldn't remember her number. I couldn't remember any of my friends' numbers. I phoned the operator, but didn't get very far because I couldn't remember their last names either. Because I didn't want to just sit there waiting for someone to happen along and help me, I figured I'd slowly make my way home. I knew it wasn't far. I turned the truck around and drove to the highway, but didn't know which way to turn. I chose left, and thankfully it was the correct choice.

It was over a week before my scrambled brains began to function normally. I'd wake up in the morning, pick up my brassiere and wonder what to do with it. I'd put it down and get dressed but forget my socks because they were out of sight in a drawer. I'd try to brush my hair with my toothbrush and curse it for being such a pathetic hairbrush. And my teeth, well they just didn't get brushed. If they did, I don't want to remember what I brushed them with!

For the most part, the good old days are gone. People breed horses these days for specific traits and good dispositions. Some breed for the characteristics of English horses — tall horses of great strength and beauty. Some breed horses specifically for working cattle in arenas — little fellows that are catty and quick, with the desire to get down and look a cow in the eye. Some breed strictly for racing — horses with unbelievable speed on a straightaway. Some for perfect conformation — horses meant to take your breath away with their regal bearing. For every discipline out there asked of a horse, someone, somewhere breeds specifically for that.

A growing number of horses are handled from birth by owners with sympathetic understanding of their physical and mental needs. It's been years since I ran across a horse who didn't know what grain in a bucket was or had never felt a rope around his neck before taking his first walk into the centre of a colt starting pen.

And that is the way it should be as we move into the future. But you know, I still miss the old days. Sometimes I even dream about them, when I'm lying in bed, with the lights out.

About the Author

Gayle Bunney grew up in Alberta, where she rode horses over Canada's vast expanse of prairie. It's a place where you can ride from sunup to sundown while you share your day with the horse beneath you, the prairie wildlife, and the contented herds of cattle grazing the land. She also spent many years riding mountain trails where she discovered a whole new offering of Mother Nature's supreme beauty. And the horse was always a part of her very existence.

From stallions to newborn foals, people-loving horses to man-hating beasts, creatures of beauty to the homely old faithful, all have found a place in her heart. Her years spent breeding, training, doctoring, and learning the subtle language spoken by the horse is her life's work.

Now residing in Bonnyville, Alberta, Gayle is content raising small breed ankle biters and top of the line quarter horses. She is the author of two other books: *Horse Stories, Riding the Wind* and *My Life with Dogs*.

RIDING ON THE WILD SIDE
Tales of Adventure in the Canadian West

"Suddenly, there was a crashing noise to our left and out of the timber came about 20 head of horses and a few bewildered elk followed by a couple of yelling cowboys."

This fascinating collection of stories is about working horses and the people who make a living riding them in Canada's mountain national parks. Imagine chasing a herd of wild horses, galloping at full speed toward an impenetrable forest ... and you get a sense of the excitement of the backcountry life.

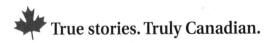True stories. Truly Canadian.

ISBN 1-55153-985-3

LEGENDARY
SHOW JUMPERS
The Incredible Stories of
Great Canadian Horses

*"He could be so gentle and quiet, but when he got
in the ring he got so excited we couldn't hold
him. ...But I wasn't afraid of him."*
Louis Welsh on Barra Lad

Once in a while a horse comes along that is
extraordinary. Air Pilot, Barra Lad, and Big Ben
have all had their turn at being the brightest star
blazing in the show-jumping sky. For more than
100 years, great Canadian high-flying horses have
provided spectators with exhilarating displays of
their jaw-dropping talent and love of jumping.

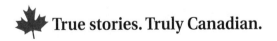 True stories. Truly Canadian.

ISBN 1-55153-980-2

STOLEN HORSES
Intriguing Tales of Rustling and Rescues

"Horse theft is on the rise...and can be traced throughout history... I found it very interesting to read about the people affected by these crimes."
Frankie Chesler, Canadian Equestrian Team Rider/Show Jumping

Dorothy Pedersen dishes up the dirt on equine crime in Canada. The horse rustling business is alive and thriving, but the valiant efforts of those who track down stolen horses are an inspiration. In this collection of true stories, the author delivers an intriguing look into this nefarious aspect of the horse world.

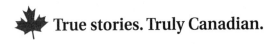 True stories. Truly Canadian.

ISBN 1-55153-971-3

OTHER AMAZING STORIES

ISBN	Title	ISBN	Title
1-55153-959-4	A War Bride's Story	1-55153-951-9	Ontario Murders
1-55153-794-X	Calgary Flames	1-55153-790-7	Ottawa Senators
1-55153-947-0	Canada's Rumrunners	1-55153-960-8	Ottawa Titans
1-55153-966-7	Canadian Spies	1-55153-945-4	Pierre Elliot Trudeau
1-55153-795-8	D-Day	1-55153-981-0	Rattenbury
1-55153-972-1	David Thompson	1-55153-991-8	Rebel Women
1-55153-982-9	Dinosaur Hunters	1-55153-995-0	Rescue Dogs
1-55153-970-5	Early Voyageurs	1-55153-985-3	Riding on the Wild Side
1-55153-798-2	Edmonton Oilers	1-55153-974-8	Risk Takers and Innovators
1-55153-968-3	Edwin Alonzo Boyd	1-55153-956-X	Robert Service
1-55153-996-9	Emily Carr	1-55153-799-0	Roberta Bondar
1-55153-961-6	Étienne Brûlé	1-55153-997-7	Sam Steele
1-55153-791-5	Extraordinary Accounts of Native Life on the West Coast	1-55153-954-3	Snowmobile Adventures
		1-55153-971-3	Stolen Horses
		1-55153-952-7	Strange Events
1-55153-992-6	Ghost Town Stories II	1-55153-783-4	Strange Events and More
1-55153-984-5	Ghost Town Stories III	1-55153-986-1	Tales from the West Coast
1-55153-993-4	Ghost Town Stories	1-55153-978-0	The Avro Arrow Story
1-55153-973-X	Great Canadian Love Stories	1-55153-943-8	The Black Donnellys
		1-55153-942-X	The Halifax Explosion
1-55153-777-X	Great Cat Stories	1-55153-994-2	The Heart of a Horse
1-55153-946-2	Great Dog Stories	1-55153-944-6	The Life of a Loyalist
1-55153-773-7	Great Military Leaders	1-55153-787-7	The Mad Trapper
1-55153-785-0	Grey Owl	1-55153-789-3	The Mounties
1-55153-958-6	Hudson's Bay Company Adventures	1-55153-948-9	The War of 1812 Against the States
1-55153-969-1	Klondike Joe Boyle	1-55153-788-5	Toronto Maple Leafs
1-55153-980-2	Legendary Show Jumpers	1-55153-976-4	Trailblazing Sports Heroes
1-55153-775-3	Lucy Maud Montgomery		
1-55153-967-5	Marie Anne Lagimodière	1-55153-977-2	Unsung Heroes of the Royal Canadian Air Force
1-55153-964-0	Marilyn Bell		
1-55153-999-3	Mary Schäffer	1-55153-792-3	Vancouver Canucks
1-55153-953-5	Moe Norman	1-55153-989-6	Vancouver's Old-Time Scoundrels
1-55153-965-9	Native Chiefs and Famous Métis		
		1-55153-990-X	West Coast Adventures
1-55153-962-4	Niagara Daredevils	1-55153-987-X	Wilderness Tales
1-55153-793-1	Norman Bethune	1-55153-873-3	Women Explorers

These titles are available wherever you buy books. If you have trouble finding the book you want, call the Altitude order desk at **1-800-957-6888**, e-mail your request to: **orderdesk@altitudepublishing.com** or visit our Web site at **www.amazingstories.ca**

New **AMAZING STORIES** titles are published every month.

GREAT DOG STORIES
Inspirational Tales About
Exceptional Dogs

*"His name is not wild dog anymore, but the
first friend, because he will be our friend for
always and always and always."*
Rudyard Kipling

Dogs have long acted as protectors, but they are
also an inspiration to many people who work
closely with them. From seeing-eye dogs to
tracking dogs, the bond formed with canine
companions can be exceptionally rewarding.
The author features the stories of nine incredi-
ble dogs and their owners.

 True stories. Truly Canadian.

ISBN 1-55153-946-2